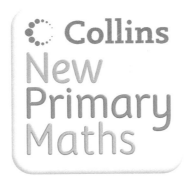

Pupil Book 4B

Series Editor: Peter Clarke

Authors: Jeanette Mumford, Sandra Roberts, Andrew Edmondson

Contents

Apples and pears

- **Add or subtract mentally pairs of two-digit numbers**

Choose one number from each basket and make 5 addition calculations and 5 subtraction calculations. Show all your working.

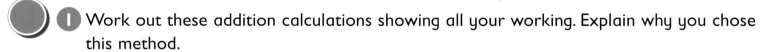

1. Work out these addition calculations showing all your working. Explain why you chose this method.

   a 76 + 48 = ☐   b 37 + 54 = ☐   c 85 + 46 = ☐   d 67 + 54 = ☐

2. Work out these subtraction calculations showing all your working. Explain why you chose this method.

   a 97 − 28 = ☐   b 85 − 36 = ☐   c 72 − 41 = ☐   d 61 − 27 = ☐

3. The difference between a pair of two-digit numbers is 13. Find 10 possible pairs of numbers. Write each pair as an addition and a subtraction calculation.

Challenge your partner.
Take turns to write a pair of two-digit numbers on a whiteboard. Challenge your partner to add them as quickly as they can in their head. They then find the difference between them. Swap roles and repeat.

You need:

- whiteboard and pen

Baking additions

● **Use written methods to add two-digit and three-digit numbers**

Write these calculations out vertically, then add the tens and then the units.

```
    4 5
+   3 3
─────
    7 0
      8
─────
    7 8
```

a 52 + 37

b 35 + 64

c 74 + 21

d 63 + 32

e 46 + 59

f 91 + 23

g 59 + 33

h 75 + 58

i 94 + 87

Write these calculations out vertically, then add the hundreds, the tens and the units.

a 168 + 75

f 512 + 93

```
    2 6 8
+     7 4
───────
    2 0 0
    1 3 0
      1 2
───────
    3 4 2
```

b 265 + 63

g 286 + 196

c 279 + 52

h 219 + 286

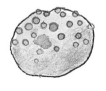

d 381 + 49

i 345 + 267

e 473 + 66

j 462 + 499

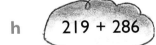

What tips would you give to someone who had not used this method before?

Subtraction highlights

- **Use written methods to subtract two-digit and three-digit numbers**

Work out these subtraction calculations, using an empty number line or the vertical method.

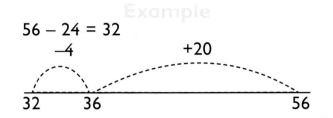

Example

$56 - 24 = 32$

-4 $+20$

32   36   56

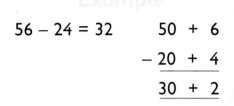

Example

$56 - 24 = 32$

```
   50 + 6
-  20 + 4
───────
   30 + 2
```

a   58 – 34 = ☐   b   87 – 43 = ☐   c   78 – 32 = ☐

d   67 – 24 = ☐   e   56 – 32 = ☐   f   49 – 23 = ☐

g   74 – 51 = ☐   h   86 – 23 = ☐   i   94 – 51 = ☐

a   176 – 53 = ☐   b   189 – 67 = ☐   c   164 – 34 = ☐

d   187 – 62 = ☐   e   247 – 71 = ☐   f   254 – 47 = ☐

g   372 – 81 = ☐   h   486 – 57 = ☐   i   438 – 91 = ☐

j   396 – 58 = ☐   k   539 – 368 = ☐   l   387 – 142 = ☐

What tips would you give to someone who has not used this method before?

Count your money

● **Relate decimals to money**

Work out the value of the coins in each row and record the amount in pounds and pence.

Remember £1 is 100p.

a

b

c

d

e

f

g

h

i

j

Convert it!

A game for 2 players.

● Take turns to point to a square on the grid.

You need:
● 10 different-coloured counters (per player)

● Your partner has to convert that amount into pounds and pence and write it down as a decimal.

● If their answer is right, they put one of their counters on that square.

● When all the grid is covered, the player with more counters on it is the winner.

524p	693p	744p	1025p	1497p
1526p	1755p	1964p	2004p	2617p
2351p	2784p	2615p	3185p	3851p
3008p	3999p	2732p	1611p	2222p

Explain what the role of the decimal point is when writing money.

524p is £5.24.

Put it in order

● **Use decimal notation for money and place money on a number line**

Copy the number lines and put the amounts on them in the correct place.

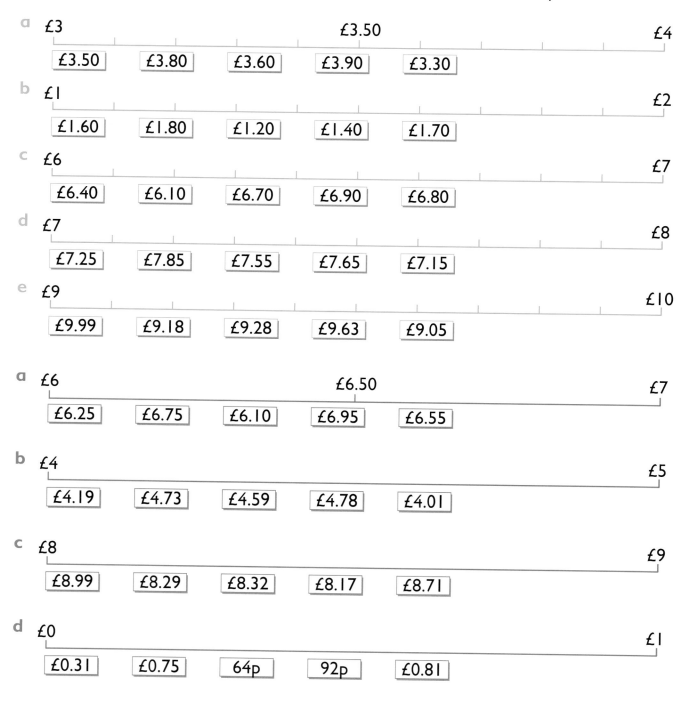

a £3   £3.50   £4

| £3.50 | £3.80 | £3.60 | £3.90 | £3.30 |

b £1   £2

| £1.60 | £1.80 | £1.20 | £1.40 | £1.70 |

c £6   £7

| £6.40 | £6.10 | £6.70 | £6.90 | £6.80 |

d £7   £8

| £7.25 | £7.85 | £7.55 | £7.65 | £7.15 |

e £9   £10

| £9.99 | £9.18 | £9.28 | £9.63 | £9.05 |

a £6   £6.50   £7

| £6.25 | £6.75 | £6.10 | £6.95 | £6.55 |

b £4   £5

| £4.19 | £4.73 | £4.59 | £4.78 | £4.01 |

c £8   £9

| £8.99 | £8.29 | £8.32 | £8.17 | £8.71 |

d £0   £1

| £0.31 | £0.75 | 64p | 92p | £0.81 |

Look at one of your number lines from the ● activity and write a new amount between each of the amounts already there.

Counting on and back

Recognise and continue patterns

Copy and complete the number sequences.

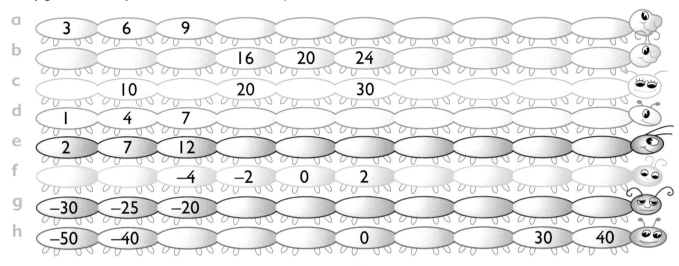

a 3 6 9

b 16 20 24

c 10 20 30

d 1 4 7

e 2 7 12

f −4 −2 0 2

g −30 −25 −20

h −50 −40 0 30 40

In each building, find out which level the car park 🚗, photocopy room 🖨, lunch room 📦, and observation gallery 🔭, are on. Use Reception or the ground floor as your starting point.

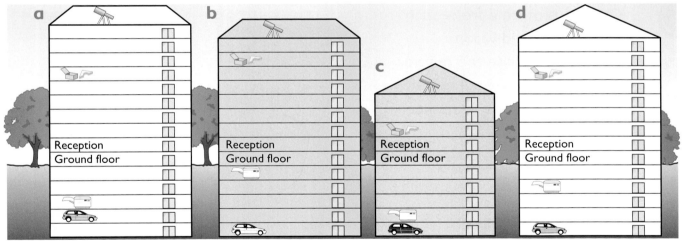

Work with a partner.

- Each person writes 5 different number sequences. Each number sequence must have 5 numbers in it and include at least two negative numbers. Make sure you know the rules for each of your number sequences, but keep them a secret from your partner.
- Swap your number sequences. Write the next 5 numbers in each of your partner's number sequences.
- When you have both finished, swap and check each other's work.

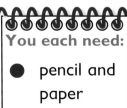

You each need:
- pencil and paper

Reviewing multiplication and division facts (1)

● **Know by heart the multiplication facts up to 10 x 10 and the related division facts**

 Multiply each of the:
- red marbles by 3 and 5
- blue marbles by 4 and 7
- green marbles by 6 and 8
- yellow marbles by 9 and 10.

Example

4 x 3 = 12
4 x 5 = 20

● Choose a marble from each jar to make a division calculation. Write the answer. Your teacher will tell you how many calculations to make.

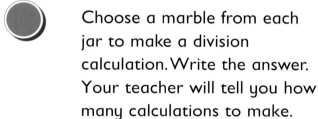

 ☐☐₁₆ means find part of the square where the product is 16, i.e. [2][8]

Now find these parts of the square.

a ☐☐₂₀ b ☐☐₅₄ c ☐☐₅₆ d ☐☐₂₁ e ☐☐₄₈

f ☐₃₆ g ☐₄₀ h ☐₁₈ i ☐₂₈ j ☐₁₄

4	5	6	8	6
7	2	8	7	3
3	4	5	10	2
6	9	3	2	4
9	2	8	7	5

Blast off 10 and 100

● Multiply or divide by 10 and 100

1 Multiply each number by 10.

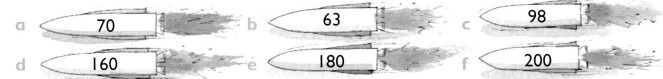

a 70   b 63   c 98

d 160   e 180   f 200

2 Divide each number by 10.

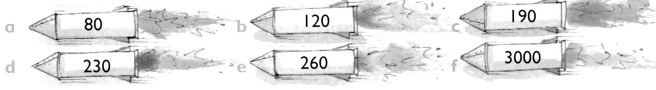

a 80   b 120   c 190

d 230   e 260   f 3000

1 Multiply each number by 10.

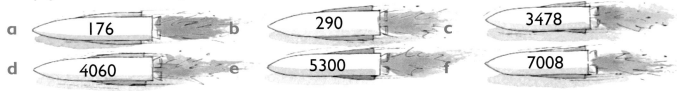

a 176   b 290   c 3478

d 4060   e 5300   f 7008

2 Divide each number by 10.

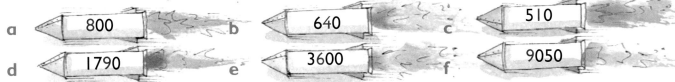

a 800   b 640   c 510

d 1790   e 3600   f 9050

3 Write the value of the red digits in question **2**.

4 A full bag contains 10 sweets.
How many bags can be filled with

a 90 sweets   b 350 sweets   c 2900 sweets   d 7040 sweets?

Each of the following calculations have either been multiplied or divided by 10 or 100. Copy and complete.

Example

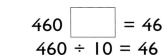

460 ☐ = 46
460 ÷ 10 = 46

a 65 ☐ = 650   b 720 000 ☐ = 7200

c 520 ☐ = 52   d 380 ☐ = 38 000

e 1200 ☐ = 12   f 265 ☐ = 2650   g 73 ☐ = 7300

h 800 ☐ = 80   i 880 ☐ = 88   j 44 500 ☐ = 445

Multiplying two-digit numbers (1)

● **Multiply a two-digit number by a one-digit number**

Example

73 × 4

Estimate 70 × 4 = 280

	70	3
4	280	12

```
   280
 +  12
 ─────
   292
```

or

```
    73
 ×   4
 ─────
   280    70 × 4
    12     3 × 4
 ─────
   292
```

Copy and complete these calculations.

a 30 × 4 =

b 90 × 5 =

c 30 × 6 =

d 80 × 3 =

e 60 × 8 =

f 80 × 7 =

g 60 × 6 =

h 20 × 6 =

i 90 × 4 =

1 Approximate the answer to each of the following. Write the calculation you used to make your estimate.

a 28 × 7 =

b 47 × 9 =

c 76 × 6 =

d 73 × 8 =

e 54 × 6 =

f 88 × 7 =

g 87 × 5 =

h 36 × 4 =

i 52 × 6 =

2 Now work out the answer to each of the calculations in question **1**.

Write down any three digits, e. g. 2, 6 and 9, and make a two-digit number and a one-digit number.
Multiply the two numbers together.
By re-arranging the three digits, investigate what other products you can make by multiplying a two-digit number by a one-digit number.
What is the largest / smallest answer you can make?

Multiplying two-digit numbers (2)

● Multiply a two-digit number by a one-digit number

Example

68×7

	60	8
7	420	56

Estimate $70 \times 7 = 490$

$$\begin{array}{r} 420 \\ + \ \ 56 \\ \hline 476 \end{array}$$

or

$$\begin{array}{r} 68 \\ \times \ \ 7 \\ \hline 420 \\ 56 \\ \hline 476 \end{array}$$

60×7
8×7

Copy and complete these calculations.

a $50 \times 6 =$

b $70 \times 3 =$

c $40 \times 7 =$

d $70 \times 4 =$

e $90 \times 5 =$

f $60 \times 4 =$

g $90 \times 7 =$

h $30 \times 9 =$

i $80 \times 8 =$

 1 Approximate the answer to each of the following. Write the calculation you used to make your estimate.

a $36 \times 3 =$

b $24 \times 7 =$

c $82 \times 5 =$

d $45 \times 6 =$

e $68 \times 4 =$

f $53 \times 9 =$

g $92 \times 8 =$

h $71 \times 9 =$

i $48 \times 7 =$

2 Now work out the answer to each of the calculations in question **1**.

Arrange each set of three-digits to make a two-digit and a one-digit number. Approximate the answer, then work out the actual answer to each calculation.

a 6 6 8

b 8 5 3

c 4 5 6

d 8 9 4

e 7 2 8

f 4 3 9

Number patterns

● **Identify and use patterns and relationships of numbers**

 1 Copy and complete the number sequences.

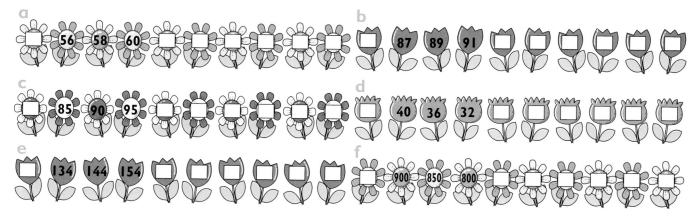

a 56 58 60

b 87 89 91

c 85 90 95

d 40 36 32

e 134 144 154

f 900 850 800

2 What is the rule for each sequence?

 1 Copy and complete the number sequences.

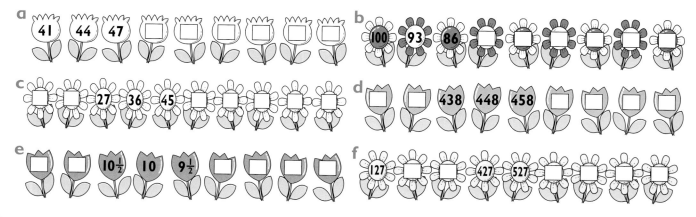

a 41 44 47

b 100 93 86

c 27 36 45

d 438 448 458

e $10\frac{1}{2}$ 10 $9\frac{1}{2}$

f 127 427 527

2 What is the rule for each sequence?

3 Make up three different number sequences using this rule: Double the number, then add 2.

 1 Paula has made up this sequence using the above rule. She thinks she has made a mistake. Can you find it?

50   102   206   412   826

Explain where she went wrong.

2 Make up a number sequence for a friend to continue. You must have at least three numbers in your sequence.

Which method?

● **Solve one-step and two-step word problems**

Work out the problems. Decide which method you are going to use. You may change the method you use depending on the calculations involved.

What is the calculation I need to do?

a   Louise timed how long she spent doing her homework one week. On Monday it took her 35 minutes and on Wednesday it took 16 minutes. How long did it take altogether?

b   Jack has £2.12 and Liz has 77p. How much do they have altogether?

c   The bookshop ordered 250 copies of a new monster book. 87 of them sell on the first day. How many are left?

d   Dan has 100 stickers. 68 are in his album and the rest are hidden in his bedroom. How many are in his bedroom?

e   A bee keeper has 165 pots of honey. He sells 71 pots of honey day. How many does he have left?

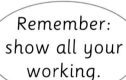

a   A machine counted how many cars drove down a street. On Saturday, it was 178 and on Sunday it was 89. The total for Saturday, Sunday and Monday was 353. How many cars drove down the street on Monday?

b   I want to buy a book that costs £5.50. I get 85p pocket money a week. I have been saving for three weeks. How much more money do I need?

Remember: show all your working.

c   There are 286 children in the assembly sitting on the floor and there are 87 sitting on chairs. 56 of the children leave the hall. How many are left?

d   The teachers have 230 biscuits in the staff room over a term. Mrs Stevens eats 41 of them. Mr Lee eats 56. Mrs Goods will not say how many she has eaten but there are 81 biscuits left. How many did she eat?

e   I have £10. I spend £2.67 on my lunch and £3.50 to get into the cinema. How much do I have left?

 Make up your own two-step word problem for a friend.

Estimating and checking

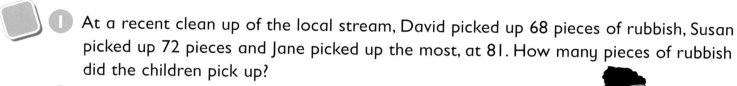

● **Solve one-step and two-step word problems**

First estimate the answer to the problem.
Then work out the answer, showing all your working.
Then check your answer.

1 At a recent clean up of the local stream, David picked up 68 pieces of rubbish, Susan picked up 72 pieces and Jane picked up the most, at 81. How many pieces of rubbish did the children pick up?

2 Mr. Adams likes to stay in shape so he runs 8 kilometres every day, Monday to Friday. At the weekend he runs 16 kilometres a day. How far does Mr. Adams run in a week?

3 In 1999, Mary's nursery class planted a six-year-old tree. Mary left the school in 2007. How old was the tree when Mary left the school?

1 Mrs. Baker teaches piano. She set a goal for Jason, one of her pupils, who does not like to practise. He has to practise 5 minutes the first night, 10 minutes the second night, 15 minutes the third night and so on. How much practice will he have done after a week?

2 The RSPCA says it costs £3 each day to keep a cat and £5 each day to keep a dog. Last week there were 10 dogs and 15 cats at the RSPCA. Mr. Crocker's Year 4 class offered to raise money to pay for one week's costs. How much will the class have to raise?

3 If you buy three cuddly bears at the supermarket it will cost you £123. If you buy just one at the local toy shop it will cost you £39. At which place is a cuddly bear cheaper?

Explain why estimating and checking answers are important.

Number investigations

● **Solve mathematical problems or puzzles, recognise and explain patterns and relationships**

What different totals can you make?
Remember to do the calculation inside the brackets first!

a (2 + 3 + 4) – 1 =

b (4 – 3) + 1 + 2 =

c (1 + 2 + 3) – 4 =

d (1 + 2 + 3) + 4 =

e (3 – 2) + 1 + 4 =

f (3 + 4 + 1) – 2 =

g (3 – 1) + 2 + 4 =

h (2 + 3) – (4 + 1) =

i (3 + 4) – (2 + 1) =

j (4 + 2) – (3 – 1) =

k (4 – 3) + (2 – 1) =

l (1 + 4) + (2 + 3) =

m (4 + 3) – (2 + 1) =

n (4 – 2) + (3 + 1) =

estigation

The children in Year 4 carried out an investigation.
Can you make 6 by using each of the digits 1, 2, 3 and 4 once and any of the operations + – × ÷?
Here are some of their results.

6
(3 + 4 + 1) – 2 = 6
(4 – 2) + 1 + 3 = 6
(21 + 3) ÷ 4 = 6
(3 × 4) ÷ (1 × 2) = 6

How many different ways of making the total 6 can you find?

estigation

Using the same digits 1, 2, 3, 4 and any of the operations + – × ÷ the children found ways of making the numbers 1 to 6. Here are their results.

1 → (3 × 2) – 4 – 1
2 → (3 + 2 + 1) – 4
3 → (21 ÷ 3) – 4
4 → (14 ÷ 2) – 3
5 → (3 × 4) ÷ 2 – 1
6 → (12 ÷ 4) + 3

Is it possible to make the numbers 7 up to 20? Record your results.

Choose any four digits from 1 to 9.
Arrange the four digits in the calculation below and solve it.

$$\left(\Box + \Box \right) \times \left(\Box + \Box \right) =$$

How many different calculations can you make by rearranging your four digits?

Finding halfway

● Make and investigate a statement about numbers

● Write the number that is halfway between these sets of numbers.

● Look carefully at each answer. What do you notice? Why has this happened?

Example

26 27
28

1

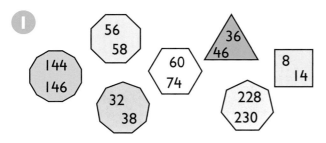

56
58

36
46

60
74

8
14

144
146

32
38

228
230

2

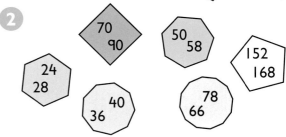

70
90

50
58

152
168

24
28

40
36

78
66

Class 4 carried out two investigations. They drew number lines to help them. This is what they found.

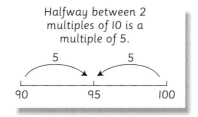

Halfway between 2 multiples of 10 is a multiple of 5.

5   5

90   95   100

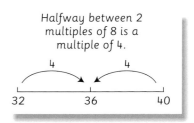

Halfway between 2 multiples of 8 is a multiple of 4.

4   4

32   36   40

1 a Use multiples of 10 to find out if what they found is always true.

b Write a statement to show what you found.

2 a Use multiples of 8 to find out if what they found is always true.

b Write a statement to show what you found.

Which numbers between 1 and 100 are multiples of 2 as well as multiples of 4? What do you notice?
What about multiples of 3 and multiples of 6?
What about multiples of 4 and multiples of 8?
What about multiples of 5 and multiples of 10?

1	2	3	4	5	6	7	8	9	10
11	12	13	14	15	16	17	18	19	20
21	22	23	24	25	26	27	28	29	30
31	32	33	34	35	36	37	38	39	40
41	42	43	44	45	46	47	48	49	50
51	52	53	54	55	56	57	58	59	60
61	62	63	64	65	66	67	68	69	70
71	72	73	74	75	76	77	78	79	80
81	82	83	84	85	86	87	88	89	90
91	92	93	94	95	96	97	98	99	100

Reviewing multiplication and division facts (2)

● **Know by heart the multiplication facts up to 10 x 10 and the related division facts**

1 Copy and complete the following multiplication calculations.

a 4 × 8 =   e 8 × 3 =   i 9 × 9 =   m 5 × 7 =

b 5 × 5 =   f 10 × 4 =   j 9 × 6 =   n 5 × 10 =

c 7 × 6 =   g 8 × 10 =   k 4 × 3 =   o 8 × 6 =

d 4 × 2 =   h 3 × 7 =   l 9 × 8 =   p 7 × 4 =

2 Copy and complete the following division calculations.

a 28 ÷ 7 =   e 16 ÷ 4 =   i 45 ÷ 5 =   m 64 ÷ 8 =

b 12 ÷ 3 =   f 36 ÷ 6 =   j 56 ÷ 8 =   n 8 ÷ 4 =

c 48 ÷ 8 =   g 27 ÷ 9 =   k 28 ÷ 7 =   o 72 ÷ 9 =

d 30 ÷ 10 =   h 20 ÷ 2 =   l 15 ÷ 3 =   p 42 ÷ 6 =

Use the colour code for each of the digits 1 to 10 to answer the following calculations.

a ☐ × ☐ = ?   b ☐ × ☐ = ?   c ☐ × ☐ = ?

d ☐ × ☐ = ?   e ☐ × 5 = ?   f ☐ × ☐ = ?

g ☐ × ☐ = ?   h ☐ × ☐ = ?   i ☐ × ☐ = ?

j 40 ÷ ☐ = ?   k 21 ÷ ☐ = ?   l 64 ÷ ☐ = ?

m 40 ÷ ☐ = ?   n 48 ÷ ? = ☐   o 63 ÷ ? = ☐

Use each set of three digits to write 2 multiplication facts and 2 division facts.

a 4   8   32   b 7   6   42   c 8   40   5

d 4   28   7   e 18   3   6   f 72   8   9

Reviewing multiplication and division facts (3)

● **Know by heart the multiplication facts up to 10 x 10 and the related division facts**

Roll the two dice and use the two numbers to make a multiplication calculation.
Multiply the two numbers together and write down the answer.
Your teacher will tell you how many calculations to make.

$2 \times 7 = 14$ $3 \times 4 = 12$
$4 \times 5 = 20$ $4 \times 7 = 28$

You need:
● 2 × 1-10 dice

A game for 2 players.

● Take turns to roll the dice to make a 2-digit number, e.g. 3, 2 could be 32 (or 23).

● The person whose turn it is places one of their counters on any number on the board that divides exactly into their dice number, i.e. 2, 4 or 8, and says the calculation: '32 divided by 4 is 8.'

● If a number cannot be divided exactly, miss a turn.

● The winner is the first person to complete a column, row or diagonal of 4 numbers.

You need:
● 2 × 0-9 dice
● 40 counters (20 of one colour, 20 of another colour)

8	3	5	4	2	9
6	7	8	8	4	5
3	6	7	5	10	6
6	4	8	3	7	4
9	2	4	9	5	8
2	6	7	5	3	3

● Choose two digits, e.g. 4 and 9.
● Multiply the two numbers together and only write down the units digit of the answer: 4, 9, 6.
● Make a list of numbers by continuing to multiply the last two digits together and writing down the units digit of the answer: 4, 9, 6, 4, 4, 6…
● Continue the list and investigate what happens.
Try starting with different pairs of numbers.

Doubling and halving

● **Double and halve two-digit numbers**

Double each of the numbers and halve each of the numbers.

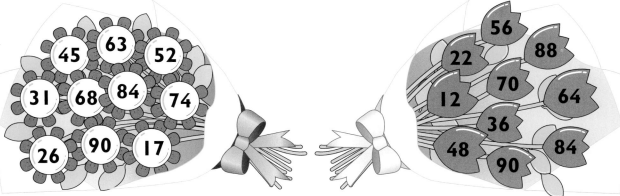

45 63 52

31 68 84 74

26 90 17

56

22 88

70

12 64

36

48 84

90

A game for 2 players.
● Take turns to roll the dice and make 2 two-digit numbers, e.g. 4 and 3 makes 43 and 34. If both of the dice numbers are odd, roll the dice again.

● Double one of the numbers and halve the other, i.e. $43 \times 2 = 86$ and $34 \div 2 = 17$.

● Follow the rules to see how many points each player wins for that round.

● The winner is the player with more points after 10 rounds.

You need:
● $2 \times 0\text{-}9$ dice
● pencil and paper

RULES

Doubled numbers:
Larger answer
wins 1 point.
Halved numbers:
Smaller answer
wins 1 point.

A game for 2 players.
● Take turns to roll the dice and make 2 two-digit numbers, e.g. 4 and 2 makes 42 and 24. If both of the dice numbers are odd, roll the dice again.

● Double one of the numbers and halve the other, i.e. $42 \times 2 = 84$ and $24 \div 2 = 12$.

● Now add both answers together, i.e. $84 + 12 = 96$. That is your score for that round.

● The winner of each round is the player with the greater total. Play 10 rounds.

You need:
● $2 \times 0\text{-}9$ dice
● pencil and paper

Doubling and halving multiples of 10

● **Double and halve two-digit and three-digit multiples of 10**

Double each of the numbers on the blue flags and halve each of the numbers on the red flags.

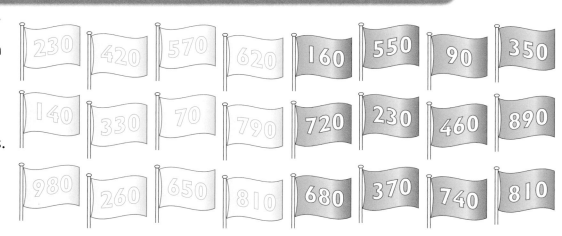

230 420 570 620 160 550 90 350

140 330 70 790 720 230 460 890

980 260 650 810 680 370 740 810

A game for 2 players.
- ● Take turns to roll the dice and make a two-digit number, e.g. 6 and 7 makes 67 (or 76).
- ● Multiply the number by 10, e.g. 67 × 10 = 670.
- ● Double and halve the number, e.g. 670 × 2 = 1340 and 670 ÷ 2 = 335.
- ● Follow the rules to see how many points each player wins for that round.
- ● The winner is the player with more points after 10 rounds.

You need:
- ● 2 × 0-9 dice
- ● pencil and paper

RULES

Doubled numbers:
Larger answer wins 1 point.
Halved numbers:
Smaller answer wins 1 point.

 1 2 3 4 5 6 7 8 9 10

Investigate
- ● Make 'doubles' using the number cards.
- ● Investigate different doubles that can be made using the cards.

You need:
- ● set of 1-10 number cards

2 and 4   3 and 6   1 3 and 2 6

Solving word problems (1)

● **Solve one-step and two-step word problems**

Read each word problem and work out the answer.

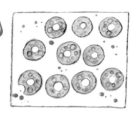

a Mrs. Smith buys 7 trays of doughnuts. How many doughnuts are there altogether?

b Julie puts 16 trays of doughnuts in the shop window. How many doughnuts are there altogether?

c Shelly buys 30 doughnuts for her class. How many trays does she buy?

d Sami orders 32 trays of doughnuts for her party. How many doughnuts are there in total?

e The baker has made a total of 250 doughnuts. How many trays does he need?

f 10 doughnuts cost £1. How much for 160 doughnuts?

a Bags of flour cost £4 each.
  i How many bags can be bought for £32?
  ii If bags of flour double in price, how many bags can be bought?

b Mr. Michael bought 3 gateaux for his dinner party. He spent £24.
  i How much did each gateau cost?
  ii How much for 6 gateaux?

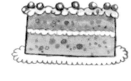

c The bakery sold 4 birthday cakes on Monday. They made £28 altogether.
  i How much for 1 cake?
  ii How much for 6 cakes?

d In one week, the bakery made £60 on chocolate biscuits. 30 packets were sold.
  i How much per packet?
  ii How much money would have been made if only 22 packets were sold?

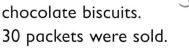

Write the different word problems for each of the following calculations.

a $(7 \times 6) + 8 = 15$
b $(8 + 2) \times 5 = 50$

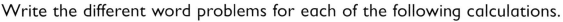

Pinboard polygons

- Draw different polygons and recognise right angles and lines of symmetry

This shape is half of a polygon.

The whole shape is

or

You need:
- I cm squared dot paper

Draw the polygons you can make with these half shapes. Find as many as you can.

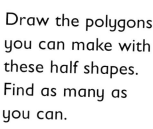

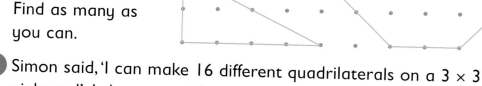
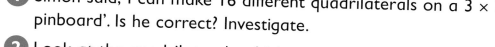

1 Simon said, 'I can make 16 different quadrilaterals on a 3 × 3 pinboard'. Is he correct? Investigate.

2 Look at the quadrilaterals which you have drawn. For each shape:

a Draw the line or lines of symmetry in red.

b Mark any right angles.

c Colour the regular shapes in blue.

Example

You need:
- ●● I cm squared dot paper
- ●● red and blue coloured pencils
- ●● ruler

1 Simon said, 'I can draw different symmetrical pentagons on a 4 × 4 pinboard'. How many could he draw? Investigate.

2 Outline some 4 x 4 pinboards on I cm square dot paper.

For each pentagon:

a Draw the line or lines of symmetry in red.

b Mark right angles.

c Colour the regular shapes in blue.

Example

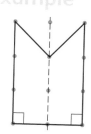

Reflecting patterns

● Reflect shapes along a line of symmetry

Copy these patterns on to squared paper. Colour the empty spaces to make them symmetrical.

a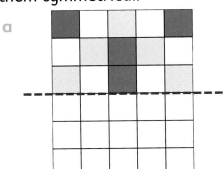

b

c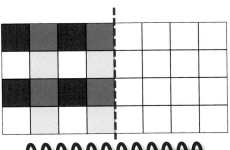

Copy these dots and mirror lines onto squared paper. Draw the reflected image of the dots.

Example

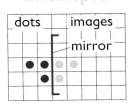

You need:

●●● 1 cm square paper
●●● ruler
●●● mirror
●●● coloured pencils

a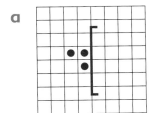

b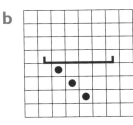

c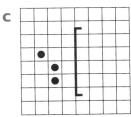

d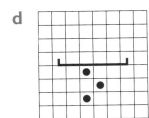

e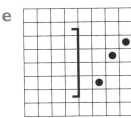

f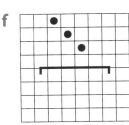

Repeat the ● activity for these patterns.

a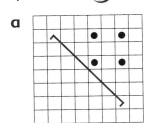

b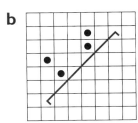

c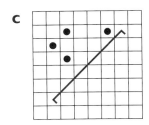

Grid patterns

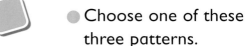

Make and describe patterns by translating a shape

- Choose one of these three patterns.
- Copy and continue it on squared paper.

Remember
You can move in any direction.

Make a pattern of your own choice on the squared paper.

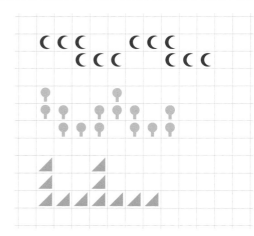

Identify the motif in these patterns.
Copy and continue each pattern on squared paper.
Colour alternate motifs.

a

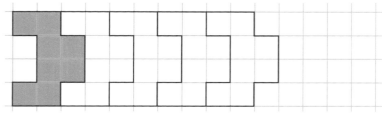

b

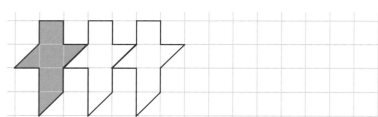

 Do the same for these grid patterns.

a

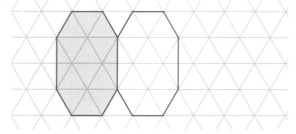

b

Working with 3-D shapes

Recognise solid shapes from drawings and build them with cubes

1 Build these solid shapes with cubes.

a 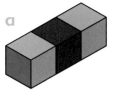   b 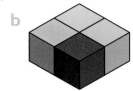   c 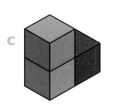   d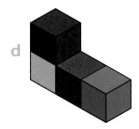

2 Take 4 cubes. Build a solid shape. Draw the plan of your shape on square dot paper.

You need:
- interlocking cubes
- I cm squared dot paper

- Work out the least number of cubes you will need to build each shape.
- Check by building each shape.
- Draw the plan of your shape on square dot paper.
- Write down the number of cubes needed.

Example

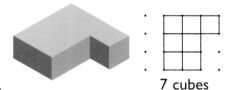

7 cubes

a 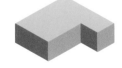   b   c

d   e    f

g    h   i

Use 5 cubes to investigate different designs for single-storey office blocks. Draw your plans on squared paper.

You need:
- interlocking cubes
- I cm squared paper
- ruler

27

Nets of open cubes

● **Recognise nets of an open cube**

1 a Make an open box with 5 square tiles.

   b Open the box to reveal the net.

   c Copy the net on to 1 cm square dot paper.

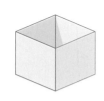

2 Repeat the steps in question **1** to find and draw two different nets for an open box.

1 You can make 12 different pentominoes.

For each pentomino:

● predict whether or not it is the net of an open cube

● make the pentomino with interlocking square tiles

● test your prediction.

Pentomino	Prediction		Test	
	Is a net	Not a net	Is a net	Not a net
a	✓		✓	
b				
c				

2 Record your results in a table.

a

b

c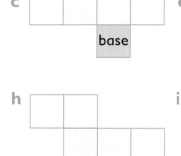

d

e

f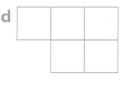

g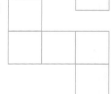

h

i

j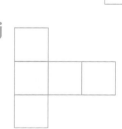

k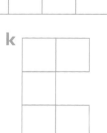

l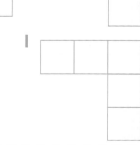

Making cubes

● Copy nets **a**, **b** and **c** from the ● activity onto 1 cm square dot paper. Rule squares 2 cm by 2 cm for each face.

● Add tabs.

● Cut out the nets.

● Assemble the open cubes, checking that the marked base is in the correct position.

Weighing – up or down

● **Measure weights in grams and kilograms)**

1 Write these weights in grams.

a $\frac{1}{2}$ kg   b 1 kg   c $\frac{1}{4}$ kg

d $\frac{3}{4}$ kg   e $\frac{1}{10}$ kg   f $2\frac{1}{2}$ kg

You need:

● balance scales
● 100 g weights
● objects to weigh

2 Find groups of
objects that weigh
about 100 g.
Make a list.

Example

12 marbles weigh
about 100 g

1 Write these weights in grams.

a 3 kg 250 g   b 5 kg 100 g   c 2 kg 750 g
d 9 kg 500 g   e 3 kg 400 g   f 4 kg 900 g

Example

3 kg 125 g = 3000 g + 125 g
= 3125 g

2 Write these weights in kilograms.

a 6500 g   b 7100 g
c 5250 g   d 8750 g

Example

3500 g = 3000 g + 500 g
= 3·5 kg

3 You have these standard weights.

100 g   200 g   500 g

What is the least number of standard weights
you can use to measure the weight of each packet?

a
b
c
d

Work with a partner.
Find the weight of one teabag
and one biscuit.

You need:

● box of teabags
● packet of
biscuits

Balancing

● **Measure weight using kilograms and grams**

This is Rita's recipe for raspberry crumble.

450 g raspberries   250 g flour   150 g sugar   100 g butter

She has these standard weights.   Write the weights she uses to measure:

100 g   200 g   50 g

a flour   b raspberries

c sugar   d butter

 1 You have a supply of these standard weights:

500 g   200 g   100 g   50 g

a Find 3 ways to balance 350 g using the 50 g, 100 g and 200 g weights.

b Find 6 ways to balance 750 g using the 4 standard weights.

350 g = 100 g + 100 g + 100 g + 50 g

2 Find ways of measuring out amounts of rice using only two standard weights.

Make drawings to show how you worked it out.

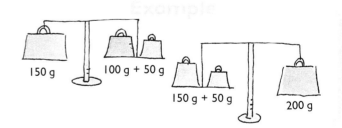

150 g   100 g + 50 g

150 g + 50 g   200 g

a Make 400 g. Use 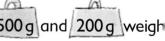 500 g and 100 g weights.   b Make 300 g. Use 500 g and 200 g weigh

c Make 450 g. Use 500 g and 50 g weights.   d Make 800 g. Use 1 kg and 200 g weights

e Make 900 g. Use 1 kg and 100 g weights.   f Make 350 g. Use 500 g and 200 g weigh

You have one 500 g and one 200 g weight. How might you measure out 900 g of rice?

Outdoors measuring

● Read scales in grams and kilograms

1 Round the weights to the nearest 10 g.

a 51 g   **b** 65 g   **c** 32 g   **d** 14 g   **e** 96 g

2 Estimate the weights of the pine cones, to the nearest 10 g.

1 Round the weights to the nearest 10 g.

a 135 g   **b** 2192 g   **c** 1845 g   **d** 3098 g   **e** 2006 g

2 Write the weight of the logs in kilograms, then in grams.

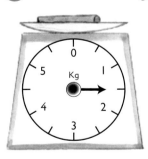   

Find the weight in grams of 1 bulb.

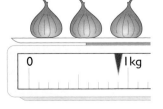 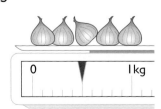 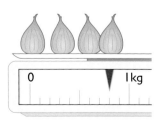 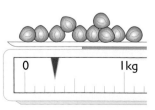

   a hyacinth   **b** tulip   **c** daffodil   **d** crocus

Sweet shop bar charts

The bar chart shows the sweets in a bag.

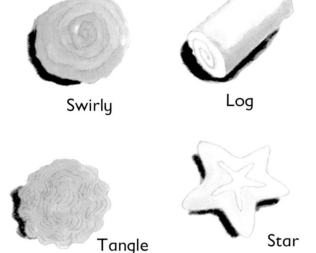

Swirly

Log

Tangle

Star

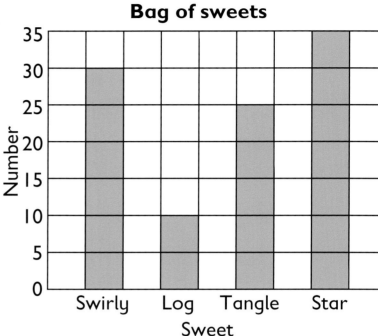

Bag of sweets

1 Use the information in the bar chart to answer these questions.

a How many Swirly sweets are there?

b Which is the least common sweet?

c There are 25 of one type of sweet. Which sweet?

d Lee took a sweet from the bag without looking. Which sweet is it most likely to be?

e Lee ate 10 Tangle sweets. How many does she have left?

f How many sweets are in a bag?

2 Copy and complete the tally chart.

Sweet	Tally	Frequency
Swirly		

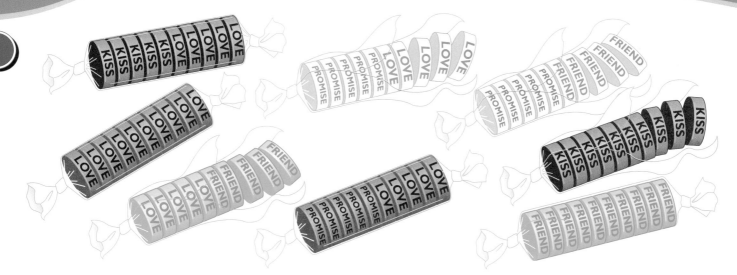

1 Copy and complete the tally chart.

Sweet	Tally	Frequency
Love Kiss Promise Friend		

You need:
- ●● squared paper
- ●● ruler
- ●● coloured pencil

2 Copy and complete the bar chart.

3 Use the information in the bar chart to answer these questions.

a Which sweet does the shop have most to sell?

b How many more Love than Kiss sweets are there?

c How many sweets are not Love sweets?

d The shop sells 10 Friend and 5 Love sweets. Which sweet is there most of now?

e How many sweets are Kiss or Friend?

f Erin bought 10 Kiss and 5 Love sweets. How many sweets are left in the shop?

Sweet words

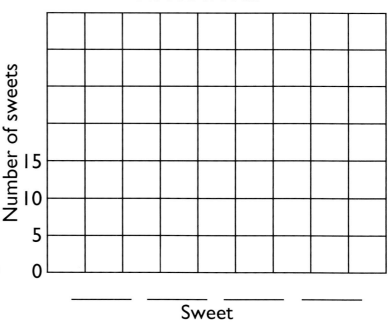

Number of sweets

15
10
5
0

Sweet

Draw a bar chart for the sweets. This time number the vertical axis 0, 10, 20 and so on.

Fairground pictograms

● **Present data in tables and pictograms**

The children in Year 4 voted for their favourite ride.

1 Copy and complete the pictogram.
Use 😊 to represent 2 votes.

2 Write three sentences about the information presented in your pictogram.

Ride	Frequency
Rollercoaster	14
House of horrors	5
Bumper cars	13
Swingboat	11

Year 4 favourite fairground rides

Rollercoaster								
House of horrors								
Bumper cars								
Swingboat								

Number of children

Key: 😊 = 2 votes

This pictogram shows the favourite rides Year 5 voted for.

Year 5 favourite fairground rides

Rollercoaster	😊	😊	😊	😊	😊	◖		
House of horrors	😊	😊	😊	😊				
Bumper cars	😊	😊	😊	😊	😊	😊	◖	
Swingboat	😊	😊	😊	😊				

Number of children

Key: 😊 = 2 votes

Use the information in the pictogram to answer these questions.

3 a How many children voted for the House of Horrors?
b Which rides were less popular than the Rollercoaster?
c How many children are there in Year 5?
d Is the most popular ride the same as for Year 4? How do you know?
e Is the least popular ride the same as for Year 4? How do you know?

The table shows how many times the children went on a ride.

1) Copy and complete the pictogram.
Use ☺ to represent 5 rides.

2) Write three sentences about the information presented in your pictogram.

Ride	Frequency
Rollercoaster	40
House of horrors	15
Bumper cars	23
Swingboat	10

Year 4 fairground rides

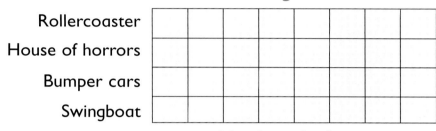

Key: ☺ = 5 rides

Number of rides

This pictogram shows how many times the children in Year 5 went on a ride.

Year 5 fairground rides

Key: ☺ = 5 rides

Number of rides

Use the information in the pictogram to answer these questions.

3) a How many rides were there on the Rollercoaster?
   b Estimate the number of rides in the House of Horrors.
   c Make a table to show the number of children for each ride.
   d Write down two sentences comparing Class Year 5 with Year 4.

Draw bar charts for the data in the activity question and the activity question (1).

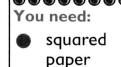
You need:
● squared paper
● ruler

35

Dog race bar chart

Dawg   Pooch   Smooch   Spot

Work in pairs.

1 Copy this score table.

2 Put the counter on Start. Roll the dice and move forward the number of spaces shown on the dice. Record the score in the table. When you reach Finish, calculate the total score for each dog.

You need:
- ●●● 1–6 dice
- ●●● a counter

Dog	Score	Total
Dawg		
Pooch		
Smooch		
Spot		

1 Copy and complete the bar chart for your scores.

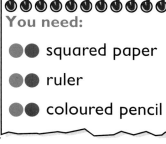

You need:
- ●● squared paper
- ●● ruler
- ●● coloured pencil

2 a Use the bar chart to answer these questions.

b What is the lowest score?

c What is the total score for Pooch and Smooch?

d Find the greatest difference between two scores.

e How many times did you land on Smooch?

Dog race results

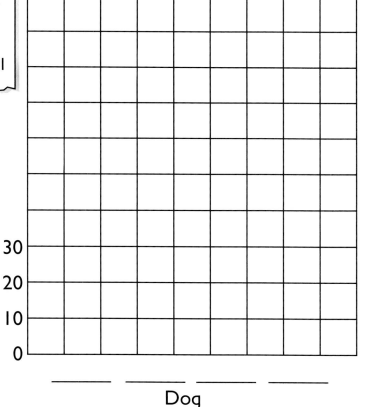

Total score — 30, 20, 10, 0

Dog

Look at the bar chart for the ⬤ activity and the table from the ⬜ activity and draw a pictogram for the data.

Counting charts

● **Present data in tables, pictograms and bar charts**

1 a Fill the space inside the red rectangle with different coloured counters.

b For each colour, make piles of ten counters.

c Copy and complete this frequency table.

d Copy and complete the pictogram. Use ◯ to represent five counters.

Colour	Frequency
Red	

You need:

● squared paper

● ruler

● counters

Coloured counters

Red

Key: ◯ = 5 counters

Number of counters

2 a How many red counters are there?

b What is the frequency for yellow counters?

c What is the highest frequency? What does this tell you?

3 Write two sentences about the information presented in your pictogram.

1 Count the coins and notes.

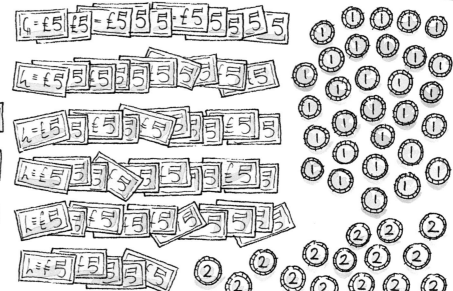

a Copy and complete the frequency table.

b Copy and complete the pictogram. Choose your own picture to represent 10 coins or notes.

Coin/Note	Frequency
£1	

You need:
● squared paper
● ruler

Coins and notes

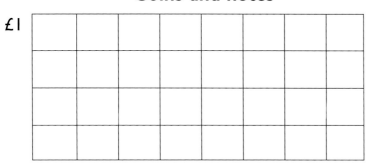

£1

Key:

Number of coins/notes

2 a How many £1 coins are there?

  b What is the frequency for £10 notes?

  c What is the highest frequency? What does this tell you?

  d How many notes are there altogether?

2 a How many £1 coins are there?

3 Write two sentences about the information presented in your pictogram.

Draw a bar chart for the data in the ⬤ activity.

Word sorting

● **Organise and present data in different ways**

These words begin with vowels.

apple   **e**xtra   **i**f   **o**ver   **u**pon

a Copy the tally chart.

b Use a reading book to find words that begin with vowels. Make a tally mark for each vowel. Stop when one letter has a frequency of between 30 and 35.

c Count the tally marks then write the frequencies.

You need:

●●● reading book

●●● squared paper ●●● ruler

●●● coloured pencils

1 Copy and complete the pictogram. Choose your own picture to represent five words.

Vowel	Tally	Frequency
a		
e		
i		
o		
u		

Vowels words begin with

a								
e								
i								
o								
u								

Key:

Number of words

2 a How many words begin with **e**?

b What is the frequency for **a**?

c What is the highest frequency? What does this tell you?

d Which vowel occurs the least?

3 Write two sentences about the information presented in your pictogram.

1 Draw two bar charts for the data from the ▢ and ⬤ activities. Give each bar chart a different scale.

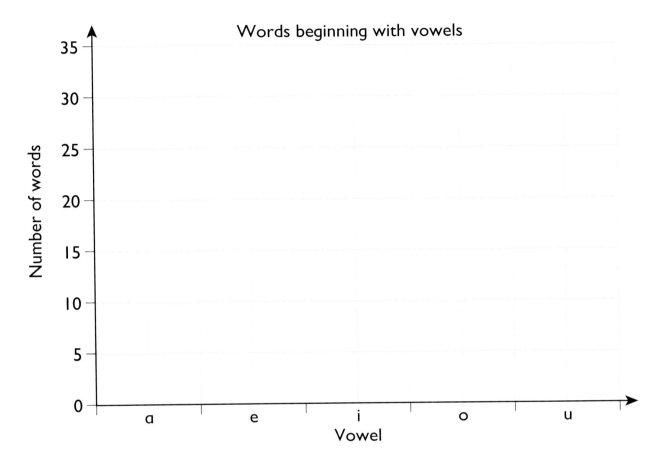

2 Which bar chart shows the data best? Explain your answer.

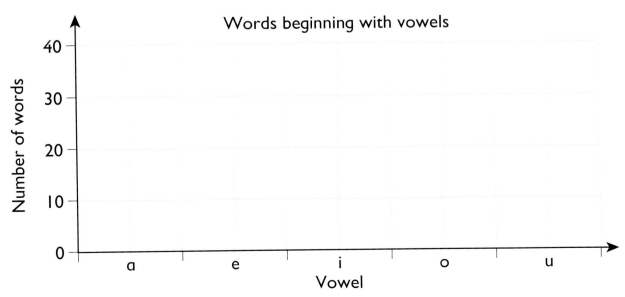

Coins and dice

● **Use Carroll diagrams to sort data**

1 Copy the Carroll diagram.

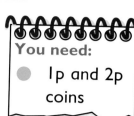

	Heads	Tails
1p coin	◯	◯
2p coin	◯	◯

2 Flip both coins together. Do this 20 times.

3 Make a cross in the Carroll diagram for each turn.

4 Write the number of crosses in each circle.

5 a Which coin got most heads?

  b How many more heads than the other coin?

  c How many heads were there altogether?

  d How many tails were there altogether?

6 Flip the coins another 20 times and draw a new Carroll diagram.

7 a Did you get more tails the first or second time?

  b Which coin showed the most tails altogether?

  c How many tails were there for both coins altogether?

8 Draw a third Carroll diagram to show all your results.

Work in pairs.

1 Copy the Carroll diagram.

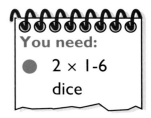

	Double	Not double
Total 6 or less	○	○
Total more than 6	○	○

2 Take turns to roll the dice.
A 'double' looks like this.

'double 4'

Record the results in the Carroll diagram.
Roll the dice ten times each. Make a tick for each result.

3 Write the number of ticks in each circle.

4 How many times did you roll a double with a total more than 6?

1 Copy the Venn diagram.

2 Record the results from the ● activity in the Venn diagram. Make a tick for each result.

3 Write the totals in the squares.

4 How many times did the dice not show a double or have a total of 6 or less?

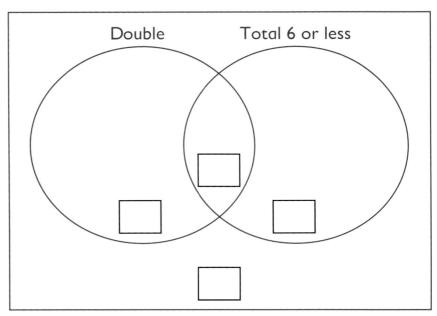

Hot and cold

● **Collect and organise information to answer a question**

Work as a group.

1 Do you think that people who prefer hot food also prefer hot drinks? Write down your prediction.

2 Ask each child in the class the following two questions.

● Which food do you eat more of at home: hot or cold?

● Which drinks do you drink more of at home: hot or cold?

Decide how you are going to collect and record the information.

Use ticks to record the children's answers in the Carroll diagram.
Write the totals in the circles.
What is your conclusion?
Was your prediction correct?

	Hot food	**Cold food**
Hot drink	◯	◯
Cold drink	◯	◯

Use ticks to complete the Venn diagram for the data you collected.

Think of another investigation about food where you could record the information you gather in a Carroll diagram.

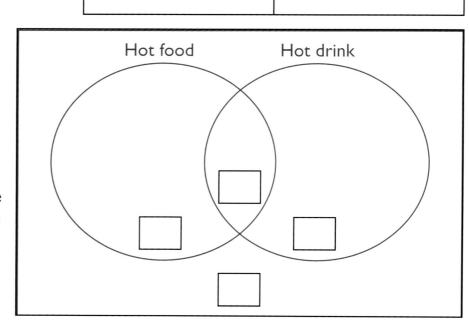

Decimal tenths

● **Use decimal notation for tenths and partition decimals**

1 Copy and complete the following number lines.

a 0   0·1   0·2   ☐   0·4   ☐   ☐   0·7   ☐   0·9   1

b 3   ☐   3·2   3·3   ☐   ☐   3·6   ☐   ☐   ☐   4

c 5   5·1   ☐   ☐   ☐   5·5   ☐   ☐   ☐   5·9   ☐

d 7   ☐   ☐   ☐   ☐   ☐   ☐   ☐   ☐   ☐   8

2 Write the decimal to one place that comes after these numbers.

a 4·2   b 5·1   c 6·8   d 3·5   e 2·4
f 9·7   g 1   h 8·3   i 4·9   j 7·6

1 Order the decimals from smallest to largest.

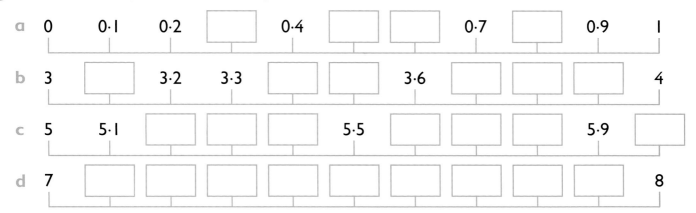

a 5·3   5·9   5·1   5   5·6   5·8   6

b 7·7   7·9   7·3   7·2   7   7·5   7·6

c 2·1   1·5   2·4   2·9   1·7   1·3   2

d 8·9   9·8   8·8   9·9   8·5   9   9·1

2 Look at question **1** c. Order the decimals from smallest to largest again, but this time write one decimal that lies between each pair of adjacent numbers.

3 Explain how you order decimals to one place.

1 What is the nearest whole number to each of these decimals?

a 7·8   b 3·2   c 4·1   d 8·9   e 1·3

2 Explain how you worked out the answers.

Carrying numbers

  Use a written method to add

Work out these calculations vertically. You will need to carry the units into the tens column.

Example

```
  345
+ 137
  482
  1
```

a 265 + 28

f 448 + 34

b 215 + 47

g 327 + 58

c 426 + 68

h 559 + 37

d 206 + 79

i 718 + 75

e 517 + 44

j 608 + 48

Remember

Add the ten you carry.

Work out these calculations vertically. You will need to carry either the tens or the units.

Example

```
  628
+ 291
  919
  1
```

a 254 + 39

f 734 + 92

b 368 + 25

g 683 + 46

c 417 + 67

h 775 + 74

d 523 + 59

i 788 + 51

e 605 + 88

j 591 + 75

Write three different types of addition calculations that you would not use the written method for and explain why.

Column subtraction

● **Use a written method to subtract**

① Copy out the calculations and work them out vertically.

a 493 − 162

b 675 − 254

c 784 − 234

d 892 − 361

e 579 − 247

Example

465
− 233
232

② These calculations need the units digit changing.

a 384 − 239

b 352 − 118

c 664 − 227

d 574 − 236

e 895 − 357

Example

6 16
2̸7̸6
− 148
128

① Copy out the calculations and work them out vertically. These calculations need the units digit changing.

a 655 − 238

b 796 − 249

c 851 − 325

d 972 − 238

e 670 − 242

Example

2 14
6̸3̸4
− 417
217

② These calculations need the tens digit changing.

a 738 − 163

b 847 − 273

c 653 − 281

d 742 − 361

e 575 − 192

Example

6 12
7̸2̸7
− 157
570

For each of the calculations from question **②** in the  activity check your answer using an addition calculation.

Multiplying two-digit numbers (3)

● **Multiply a two-digit number by a one-digit number**

Example

68 × 7

Estimate

70 × 7 = 490

	60	8
7	420	56

```
  420
+  56
  476
```

or

```
   68
 ×  7
  420    60 × 7
   56     8 × 7
  476
```

Copy and complete.

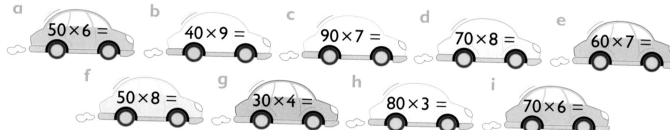

a 50 × 6 =   b 40 × 9 =   c 90 × 7 =   d 70 × 8 =   e 60 × 7 =

f 50 × 8 =   g 30 × 4 =   h 80 × 3 =   i 70 × 6 =

1 Approximate the answer to each of the following. Write the calculation you used to make your estimate.

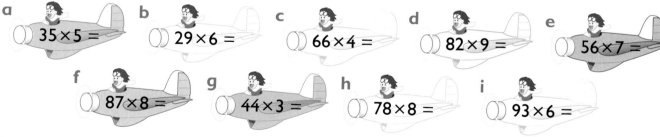

a 35 × 5 =   b 29 × 6 =   c 66 × 4 =   d 82 × 9 =   e 56 × 7 =

f 87 × 8 =   g 44 × 3 =   h 78 × 8 =   i 93 × 6 =

2 Now work out the answer to each of the calculations in question **1**.

Use a written method to work out the answer to these calculations. Be sure to make an estimate first.

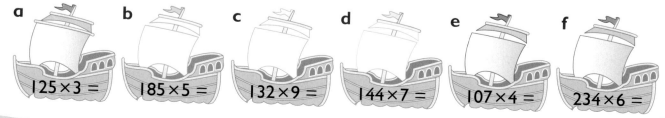

a 125 × 3 =   b 185 × 5 =   c 132 × 9 =   d 144 × 7 =   e 107 × 4 =   f 234 × 6 =

Solving word problems (2)

● Solve one-step and two-step word problems

Read each word problem and work out the answer.

a John buys 7 climbing plants.
  How much does he spend?

b What is the total cost of 9 packs of
  garden tools?

c Mr. Jones has £65. Does he have enough
  money to buy 6 climbing plants?

d How many terracotta pots can you
  buy with £90?

e Josie buys the last two garden hoses.
  How much does she spend?

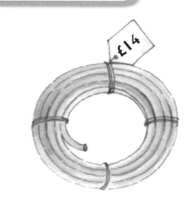

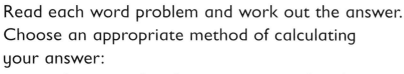

Read each word problem and work out the answer.
Choose an appropriate method of calculating
your answer:

• mental   • mental with jottings   • pencil and paper

a John buys 2 garden manuals. How much does he spend?

b Mrs. Clarke buys 4 climbing plants. Mr. Clarke buys
  6 terracotta pots. Who spends more money? How
  much more?

c The garden shop has 37 rose bushes to sell. How much
  money will they make?

d Jim, the gardener, has enough money to buy 57 packets
  of seeds. How much money does he have?

e Joanna has £100. She buys 24 packets of seeds
  and 2 packets of tools. What else can she buy
  with her change?

Choose two problems from the ● activity and
check your answers. Show all your working.

Cookhouse problems

● **Know the relationships between units of weight**

1 Work out what each lunch weighs.

a b c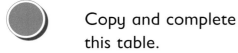

Weights of food			
hamburger	125g	apple	150g
sandwiches	150g	orange	250g
baked potato	250g	banana	175g
quiche	75g	drink	250g
crisps	25g		

2 Write which lunch is: a just over $\frac{1}{2}$ kg   b nearly $\frac{3}{4}$ kg   c about $\frac{1}{4}$ kg

Copy and complete this table.

Weight of 1 item		Number of servings			Total weight of 10	
		2	**4**	**10**	**kg and g**	**kg**
hamburger	125 g	250 g	500 g	1250 g	1 kg 250 g	1·25 kg
quiche	75 g					
baked potato	250 g					
sandwiches	150 g					
banana	175 g					

Work as a group to investigate the strength of paper shapes.

a   b   c d

 cut
off

You need:

● sheets of A4 paper
● scissors
● ruler
● sticky tape
● 10 cm square of card
● supply of 50 g weights

● On a sheet of A4 paper measure and mark a 1 cm strip to form a flap.
● Roll the paper to form a cylinder and stick down the flap.
● Place the square card on top of the cylinder. Put 50 g weights on the card until the cylinder collapses. Write the weight the cylinder supported before collapsing.
● Repeat for a square-based and a triangular-based shape.

Weights work-out

● **Solve problems involving weight**

1 Look at these eggs.

Write which egg is the best buy.

a at £2.99

b at £1.99

£1.99 115g A

£1.99 90g B

C

£2.99 209g

D

£2.99 179g E

£1.99 136g

2 What is the difference in weight between:

a the lighter and the heavier item at £1.99?   b the lighter and heavier item at £2.99?

1 What is the approximate weight in grams of:

a 1 potato   b 1 chicken thigh   c 1 pepper   d 1 onion   e 1 tub of yoghurt?

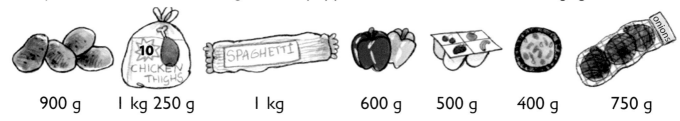

900 g   1 kg 250 g   1 kg   600 g   500 g   400 g   750 g

2 a How much heavier is the bag of chicken thighs than the packet of spaghetti?

b How much lighter are the peppers than the onions?

3 The quiche is for 5 people. Roughly how many grams are in one portion?

4 How much spaghetti is left after 4 people each have a 90 g serving?

5 Work out in kilograms, the total weight of food in each wire basket.

a   b   c   d

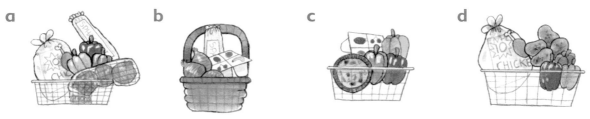

You have a bag of rice and a packet of pasta. Together they weigh 3·5 kg. The rice weighs 2 kg more than the pasta. What does the pasta weigh?
What if the total weight is 4·5 kg? What if the rice weighs 2·5 kg more than the pasta?

Pinboard perimeters

● **Calculate the perimeter of rectangles and other simple shapes**

 1 Make these rectangles on your pinboard.

2 Count the number of units around the edge to find the perimeter.

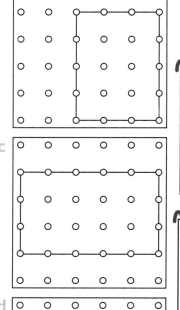

Example

4 + 3 + 4 + 3
is 14 units

You need:
● pinboard
● elastic bands

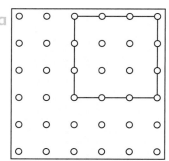 a

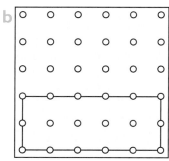 b

c

d

1 Use your pinboard to find the following and record each one on 1 cm dot paper.

  a 2 rectangles with a perimeter of 12 units
  b 3 rectangles with a perimeter of 18 units.

2 a Make these shapes with 5 square tiles.

You need:
● pinboard
● elastic bands
● 1 cm squared dot paper
● ruler
● 5 square tiles
● coloured pencil

i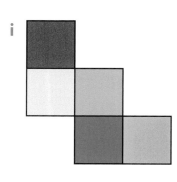
ii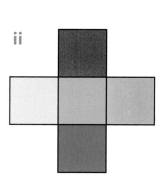
iii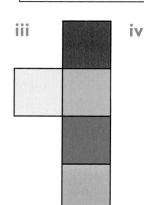
iv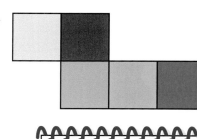

  b Find the perimeter of each shape.

  a Make different shapes with 5 square tiles.
  b Draw each shape on 1 cm dot paper and find its perimeter in centimetres.
  c Colour the shapes that have the same perimeter.

You need:
● 5 square tiles
● ruler
● coloured pencils
● 1 cm squared dot paper

Compass points

● **Use the eight compass directions**

Tom made this map of the places he visited in Austin, Texas.
Write what is:

a West of The Capitol

b North of the
  Governor's Mansion

c East of the Driskill Hotel

d South of Ninfa's Mexican food.

You are at the top of The Capitol.
Which building is:

a i to the SW?

   ii to the NE?

   iii to the NW?

b Face the Longhorns
  Football Stadium.
  Turn clockwise through 90°
  then 45°.

   i In which direction do you
      now face?

   ii Which building do you see?

c Face Austin Airport. Turn
  anti-clockwise to face Allen's
  Boots Store. How many degrees do you turn through?

d i Name the buildings you see as you turn clockwise from S to NW.

   ii Through how many degrees do you turn?

e i In which direction are you facing if you see Bark 'n' Purr?

   ii Which building lies in the opposite direction?

Work with a partner.
Using the map of Austin, take turns to give instructions
to your partner that involve making and measuring
clockwise and anti-clockwise turns.

> I am at the
> Football Stadium facing
> The Capitol. I turn 45° in
> an anti-clockwise direction.
> Which building am I
> facing now?

Measuring angles

● **Draw and measure angles of 90°, 60°, 45° and 30°**

The Zuni Indians use the rain bird motif to decorate their pottery.

A rain bird has a hook-like head, a triangular body, two legs and three feathers.

① Use your set square to measure the size of each angle.

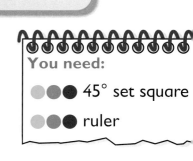

You need:
●●● 45° set square
●●● ruler

Record the size of the angle at the head, tail and body.

Example

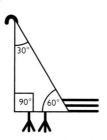

head angle = 30°
tail angle = 60°
body angle = 90°

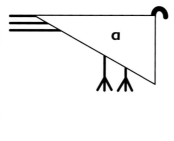

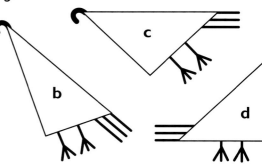

② Use your set squares to design your own rain bird. Draw it in your exercise book. Measure and mark the size of each angle.

① Copy and complete these sentences. Write > or < in the blank space.

  a 60° ☐ 45°   b 45° ☐ 30°   c 45° ☐ 90°

  d 90° ☐ 60°   e 45° + 30° ☐ 90°   f 60° + 45° ☐ 90°

② Use a ruler and a set square to draw a triangle with:

  a 2 angles of 45°

  b 2 angles of 60°

  c 1 angle of 45°, 1 angle of 60°

  d 1 angle of 60°, 1 angle of 30°

  e 1 angle of 30°, 1 angle of 45°.

Using your set square, measure and record the size of the third angle for each triangle in ● question ② .

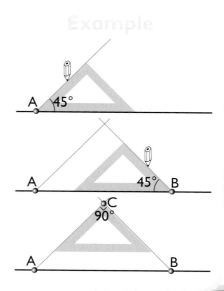

Example

Reviewing multiplication and division facts (4)

● **Know by heart the multiplication facts up to 10 x 10 and the related division facts**

Choose an apple and an orange to make a multiplication calculation. Write the answer. Your teacher will tell you how many calculations to make.

Apples: 5, 10, 3, 6, 8, 9, 4, 7

Oranges: 5, 6, 8, 2, 4, 9, 7, 3

Divide each of the:
● oranges by 3 and 6
● pears by 2, 4 and 8
● apples by 6 and 9
● bananas by 5 and 10
● melons by 7.

Example

$6 \div 3 = 2$

$6 \div 6 = 1$

42, 32, 50, 16, 18, 21, 8, 54, 56, 24, 20, 30, 6, 36

| 0 | 1 | 2 | 3 | 4 | 5 | 6 | 7 | 8 | 9 | 10 | ÷ | = |

Investigate how many different division calculations you can make using the digit cards.

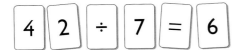

$4\ 2 \div 7 = 6$ $7\ 2 \div 9 = 8$

You need:
● set of 0-9 digit cards
● division (÷) symbol cards
● equals (=) symbol cards

Reviewing multiplication and division facts (5)

● **Know by heart the multiplication facts up to 10 x 10 and the related division facts**

 1 Copy and complete the table.

x	8	6	2	7	9	5	10	4
2	16							
4								
3								

2 Copy and complete.

a 16 ÷ 4 =   b 12 ÷ 2 =   c 50 ÷ 5 =   d 18 ÷ 3 =

e 70 ÷ 10 =   f 27 ÷ 3 =   g 45 ÷ 5 =   h 28 ÷ 4 =

3 Copy and complete.

a 18 ÷ ☐ = 3   b 2 × ☐ = 8   c ☐ ÷ 8 = 2   d 10 × ☐ = 90

e ☐ × 4 = 20   f 30 ÷ ☐ = 6   g 7 × ☐ = 21   h ☐ ÷ 2 = 10

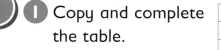 **1** Copy and complete the table.

x	5	7	3	4	6	8	5	9
6	30							
9								
8								
7								

2 Copy and complete.

a 21 ÷ 7 =   b 12 ÷ 6 =   c 49 ÷ 7 =   d 63 ÷ 9 =

e 36 ÷ 6 =   f 27 ÷ 9 =   g 72 ÷ 8 =   h 80 ÷ 8 =

3 Copy and complete.

a ☐ × 8 = 64   b 6 × ☐ = 42   c ☐ ÷ 4 = 4   d 48 ÷ ☐ = 6

e 24 ÷ ☐ = 8   f ☐ ÷ 9 = 4   g 9 × ☐ = 45   h 7 × ☐ = 49

Use the clues to find the numbers.

a Multiply me by 9 and the answer is 72.

b I am the eighth multiple of 6.

c I am the result of multiplying 4 and 7.

d When I am multiplied by myself the answer is 36.

e I am a multiple of 8, between 10 and 20.

f I am the only two-digit multiple of 7 and 9.

g I am a multiple of 4. I am less than 50.

Using multiplication facts

● **Use multiplication facts up to 10 x 10 to work out related facts**

Copy and complete.

a 8 x 6 =   f 7 x 6 =   k 5 x 8 =

b 6 x 6 =   g 4 x 3 =   l 9 x 4 =

c 4 x 4 =   h 4 x 9 =   m 4 x 6 =

d 6 x 3 =   i 8 x 3 =   n 7 x 9 =

e 3 x 9 =   j 9 x 2 =   o 8 x 2 =

1 Copy and complete each set of calculations.

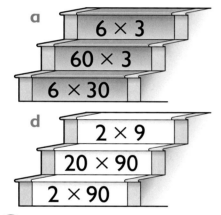

a
6 × 3
60 × 3
6 × 30

b
4 × 8
4 × 80
40 × 80

c
7 × 3
7 × 30
70 × 3

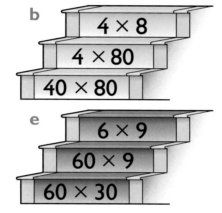

d
2 × 9
20 × 90
2 × 90

e
6 × 9
60 × 9
60 × 30

f
5 × 8
50 × 80
5 × 80

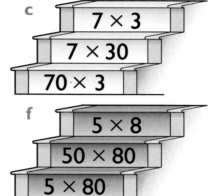

2 Use your knowledge of the times tables facts up to 10 x 10 to help you work out the answers to these calculations.

a 8 x 30 =   e 20 x 80 =   i 80 x 90 =

b 20 x 40 =   f 50 x 70 =   j 9 x 60 =

c 3 x 90 =   g 90 x 40 =   k 80 x 3 =

d 70 x 3 =   h 50 x 2 =   l 70 x 30 =

Copy and complete.

a 90 x ☐ = 180   e 70 x ☐ = 490   i ☐ x 70 = 5600

b ☐ x 80 = 320   f ☐ x 90 = 2700   j ☐ x 30 = 180

c ☐ x 80 = 3200   g 40 x ☐ = 2000   k 20 x ☐ = 180

d ☐ x 40 = 280   h ☐ x 80 = 3200   l 30 x ☐ = 1800

Multiplying two-digit numbers (4)

● **Multiply a two-digit number by a one-digit number**

- Choose one number from each team to make a multiplication calculation.
- Approximate the answer first and write it down.
- Then use a written method to work out the answer.
- Your teacher will tell you how many different multiplication calculations to make.

Example

55 × 8

Estimate

60 × 8 = 480

	50	5
8	400	40

$$\begin{array}{r} 400 \\ + \ \ 40 \\ \hline 440 \end{array}$$

or

$$\begin{array}{r} 55 \\ \times \ \ 8 \\ \hline 400 \\ 40 \\ \hline 440 \end{array}$$

50 × 8
5 × 8

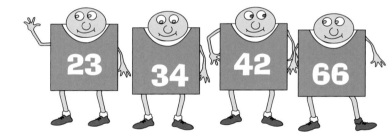

Easy elevens

To multiply by 11, multiply by 10 and adjust

Multiply the number on each balloon by 10.

  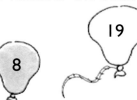 

15　　8　　19　　22　　13　　18　　25

Example

$16 \times 10 = 160$

Multiply the number on each balloon by 11. Show your working.

HINT

Multiply by 10 first then add.

Example

13

$$13 \times 11 = (13 \times 10) + 13$$
$$= 130 + 13$$
$$= 143$$

a

5

b

14

c

20

d

26

e

19

Use the same method to multiply each of these numbers by 11.

a　37　　　　b　68　　　　c　94　　　　d　134　　　e　274

Cooking fractions

● **Find fractions of numbers and amounts**

Example

$16 \div 4 = 4$
$= \frac{1}{4}$ of $16 = 4$

Work out these division facts.
Then write each fact as a fraction calculation.

a $15 \div 5$

b $80 \div 10$

c $40 \div 5$

d $120 \div 10$

e $45 \div 5$

f $700 \div 10$

g $35 \div 5$

h $950 \div 10$

 1 Find $\frac{1}{5}$ of each item of food. Then write your answer as a division fact.

a  30 g

b  25 ml

c  500 g

2 Find $\frac{1}{10}$ of each item of food. Then write your answer as a division fact.

a  70 g

b  300 ml

c  1 kg

3 Match each fraction of £1 with a coin.

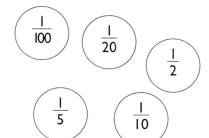

$\frac{1}{100}$ $\frac{1}{20}$ $\frac{1}{2}$ $\frac{1}{5}$ $\frac{1}{10}$

a

b

e

c

d

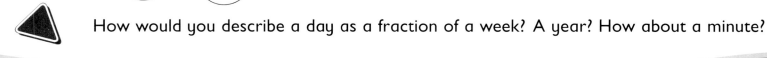

How would you describe a day as a fraction of a week? A year? How about a minute?

Fraction problems

● Find fractions of numbers and amounts

a There are 25 pupils in the class. $\frac{1}{5}$ of the pupils support Chelsea Football Club and the remainder support Arsenal. How many pupils support Arsenal?

b The local shop normally sells cereal bars for 40p. The shopkeeper says I can buy them for $\frac{1}{4}$ less than the normal price. How much can I buy a cereal bar for?

c Billy collected 36 conkers but lost $\frac{3}{4}$ of them on his way to school through a hole in his bag. When he arrived at school, how many conkers did Billy have left?

a Dan is 160 cm tall and his brother Ben is $\frac{3}{4}$ as tall as him. How tall is Ben?

b The weather forecaster says that it is 20°C in London but only $\frac{7}{10}$ as hot in New York. How hot is it in New York?

c Skateboards cost £36 each in my local store. The shopkeeper says if I buy one, I can buy another for only $\frac{7}{9}$ of the normal price. How much would a second skateboard cost?

The café sells milkshakes in two sizes. A small milkshake contains 300 ml and a large milkshake contains $\frac{2}{3}$ more.

a How much does a large milkshake contain?

b If Mr. Jones drinks $\frac{2}{3}$ of a small milkshake and Ms. Wise $\frac{1}{2}$ of a large milkshake, who drinks the most?

Make it equal

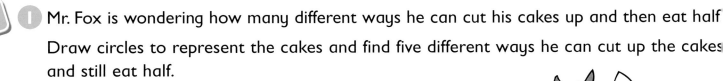

● **Use diagrams to identify fractions that are the same**

1 Mr. Fox is wondering how many different ways he can cut his cakes up and then eat half

Draw circles to represent the cakes and find five different ways he can cut up the cakes and still eat half.

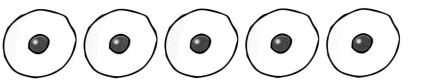

2 Mr. Rabbit is wondering how many different ways he can cut his cakes up and then eat one quarter.

Draw circles to represent the cakes and find five different ways he can cut up the cakes and still eat one quarter.

1 The fox cub triplets are arguing about how many ways they can divide the cake up equally on their birthday.

How many ways can you find? Draw circles to represent the cake.

2 Mr. Hare is feeling extremely hungry and wants to eat $\frac{3}{4}$ of all the cakes at the party. How many different ways can you find to cut up the cakes so that he will be able to ea $\frac{3}{4}$? Draw circles to represent the cakes and show your answers.

Explain how you would work out one of the ● activity questions without using picture or diagrams.

Fraction walls

● **Use diagrams to identify fractions that are the same**

1 Copy and complete the halves fraction wall. Divide each row into the labelled fraction.

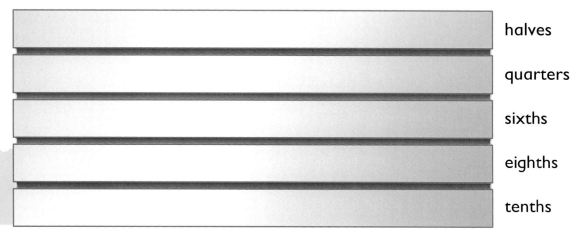

halves

quarters

sixths

eighths

tenths

2 Now write all the equivalent fractions for $\frac{1}{2}$.

1 Copy and complete the quarters fraction wall. Divide each row into the labelled fraction.

thirds

quarters

sixths

eighths

ninths

tenths

twelfths

2 Now write all the equivalent fractions for $\frac{1}{4}$ and then $\frac{3}{4}$.

What other equivalent fractions
can you see in the wall?

One fraction

● **Identify pairs of fractions that total 1**

  1 Meg has cut her cake into 8 equal pieces. How many different ways can you complete this calculation?

$$\frac{\square}{8} + \frac{\square}{8} = \frac{8}{8}$$

2 Explain why $\frac{8}{8}$ is the same as one whole.

1 Explain how you know when a fraction is equal to one whole.

2 Martin has cut his cake into 10 equal pieces.

How many ways can you complete this calculation?

$$\frac{\square}{10} + \frac{\square}{10} = \frac{10}{10}$$

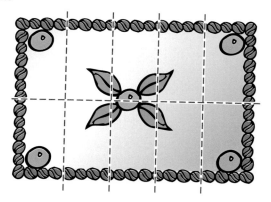

 How many ways can you complete the following calculation?

$$\frac{\square}{9} + \frac{\square}{9} = \frac{8}{9}$$

Lolly fractions

● **Understand mixed numbers**

Write the number of lolly packs.

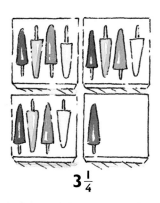

$3\frac{1}{4}$

a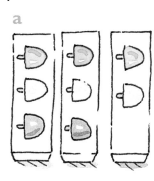

b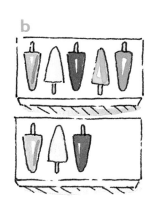

c

1 Match each fraction to the lolly packs. $1\frac{4}{5}$ $2\frac{3}{4}$ $2\frac{3}{8}$ $1\frac{4}{10}$

a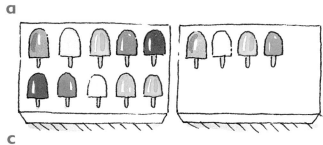

b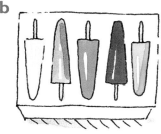

c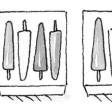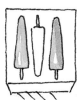

d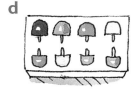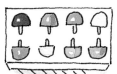

2 This is a whole pack of ice cream.
Draw these numbers of packs.

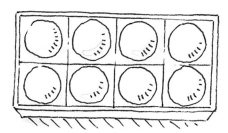

a $2\frac{1}{2}$ b $3\frac{1}{4}$ c $1\frac{3}{8}$

d $2\frac{3}{4}$ e $3\frac{7}{8}$ f $1\frac{1}{4}$

Write 5 mixed numbers between 1 and 2, in order starting with the smallest

More mixed numbers

● **Understand mixed numbers and position them on a number line**

Draw the number lines and write these mixed numbers in the correct place.

a $1\frac{1}{2}$ $2\frac{1}{2}$ $3\frac{1}{2}$ $4\frac{1}{2}$

b $1\frac{1}{4}$ $2\frac{1}{4}$ $3\frac{1}{4}$ $3\frac{3}{4}$

c $1\frac{1}{3}$ $2\frac{1}{3}$ $3\frac{1}{3}$ $4\frac{2}{3}$

d $1\frac{1}{5}$ $1\frac{3}{5}$ $2\frac{4}{5}$ $2\frac{2}{5}$

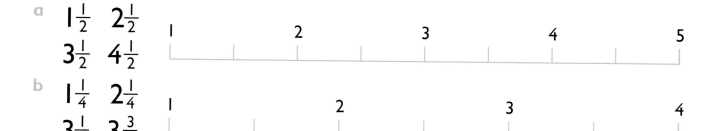

a $3\frac{1}{2}$ $3\frac{1}{4}$ $3\frac{3}{4}$ $4\frac{1}{2}$ $4\frac{3}{4}$

b $2\frac{3}{5}$ $2\frac{1}{5}$ $3\frac{4}{5}$ $3\frac{2}{5}$ $2\frac{2}{5}$

c $4\frac{2}{6}$ $4\frac{3}{6}$ $4\frac{5}{6}$ $5\frac{3}{6}$ $5\frac{4}{6}$

d Choose your own five mixed numbers to go on this number line.

6   7   8   9

Explain how to position mixed numbers on a number line.

66

Fractions and decimals

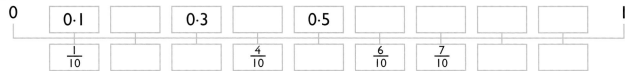

● **Recognise decimals and fractions that are the same**

1 Copy and complete the number line.

0 | 0·1 | | 0·3 | | 0·5 | | | | | 1
| $\frac{1}{10}$ | | | $\frac{4}{10}$ | | $\frac{6}{10}$ | $\frac{7}{10}$ | | |

2 Write the matching decimal and fraction.

Example

$\frac{3}{10}$ = 0·3

a $\frac{7}{10}$ = ☐

b ☐ = 0·1

c ☐ = 0·9

d $\frac{5}{10}$ = ☐

e ☐ = 0·2

f $\frac{4}{10}$ = ☐

3 Write the matching decimal and fraction.

a $2\frac{3}{10}$ = ☐

b $1\frac{8}{10}$ = ☐

c ☐ = 4·5

d ☐ = 9·2

e $5\frac{1}{10}$ = ☐

f ☐ = 15·4

g ☐ = 1·2

h $2\frac{7}{10}$ = ☐

i $4\frac{1}{10}$ = ☐

1 Write these amounts using pounds and pence.

a 70p = £0·70

b 40p = £

c $\frac{5}{10}$ of £1 = £

d 60p = £

e $\frac{9}{10}$ of £1 = £

f 10p = £

g 20p = £

h $\frac{8}{10}$ of £1 = £

i $\frac{10}{10}$ of £1 = £

2 Change these lengths to centimetres.

a 0·7 m = 70 cm

b $\frac{3}{10}$ m =

c 0·4 m =

d 0·60 m =

e $\frac{5}{10}$ m =

f 2·2 m =

g $1\frac{9}{10}$ m =

h $2\frac{8}{10}$ m =

i 3·6 m =

Remember

$\frac{1}{10}$ = 0·1 = 10 cm

Explain why $\frac{1}{10}$ and 0·1 are equivalent.

More fractions and decimals

- **Recognise decimals and fractions that are the same**

 1 Copy and complete the table.

decimal	0·1		0·25		0·4		0·6		0·75		0·9
fraction		$\frac{2}{10}$		$\frac{3}{10}$		$\frac{1}{2}$		$\frac{7}{10}$		$\frac{8}{10}$	

2 Write the matching decimal and fraction.

a $2\frac{3}{10} = 2·3$

b $1\frac{1}{2} = $ ☐

c $5\frac{1}{4} = $ ☐

d ☐ $= 3·9$

e ☐ $= 6·5$

f ☐ $= 1·75$

g $1\frac{1}{10} = $ ☐

h $9\frac{3}{4} = $ ☐

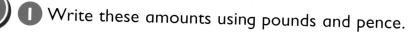

1 Write these amounts using pounds and pence.

a $\frac{6}{10}$ of £1 = £0·60

b $\frac{2}{10}$ of £1

c $\frac{3}{4}$ of £1

d $\frac{1}{2}$ of £1

e $\frac{1}{4}$ of £1

f $\frac{7}{10}$ of £1

2 Write these amounts as fractions of £1.

a 20p = $\frac{2}{10}$ of £1

b 25p

c 90p

d 75p

e 10p

f 50p

3 Change these lengths to centimetres.

a 0·7 m

b 0·25 m

c $\frac{1}{2}$ m

d 2·2 m

e $1\frac{3}{4}$ m

f 4·9 m

Write these in order from smallest to largest.

a $\frac{7}{10}$ of £1, £0·65, 60p, $\frac{3}{4}$ of £1

b $\frac{3}{10}$ m, 0·2 m, $\frac{1}{4}$ m, 0·28 m

c 1·3 m, 120 cm, $1\frac{1}{4}$ m, $1\frac{4}{10}$ m

d 435 cm, 4·2 m, $4\frac{3}{4}$ m, 4·60 m

Lottery fractions

● Represent a puzzle or problem using number sentences or diagrams

Lucky Jim won the lottery.

Here is a diagram to show how he spent his winnings.

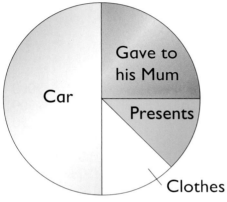

He won £6000. Work out how much he spent on each thing. Show all your working.

Unlucky Jill said, 'If I won the lottery I would spend $\frac{3}{6}$ on a holiday, $\frac{2}{6}$ on my friends and give the rest to charity.'

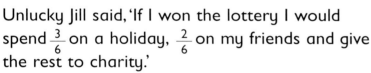

a Draw a diagram to show how she would spend her winnings.
b What fraction would she give to charity?
c What is another fraction that would describe how much she would spend on a holiday?

Fortunate Fred won the lottery.
He spent $\frac{2}{8}$ of his winnings on a big party. He spent half of what he had left on a swimming pool. What he had left he divided equally between a charity, his mum and his granny. His granny got £10 000.

a Draw a diagram to represent his winnings.
b How much did he spend on each thing?
c What fraction of his winnings did he spend on each thing?

Make up a problem about Lucky Lucy and her lottery win.

Maths Facts

Problem solving

The seven steps to problem solving

1 Read the problem carefully. **2** What do you have to find?

3 What facts are given? **4** Which of the facts do you need?

5 Make a plan. **6** Carry out your plan to obtain your answer. **7** Check your answer.

Number

Positive and negative numbers

−10 −9 −8 −7 −6 −5 −4 −3 −2 −1 0 1 2 3 4 5 6 7 8 9 10

Place value

1000	2000	3000	4000	5000	6000	7000	8000	9000
100	200	300	400	500	600	700	800	900
10	20	30	40	50	60	70	80	90
1	2	3	4	5	6	7	8	9
0·1	0·2	0·3	0·4	0·5	0·6	0·7	0·8	0·9
0·01	0·02	0·03	0·04	0·05	0·06	0·07	0·08	0·09

Number facts

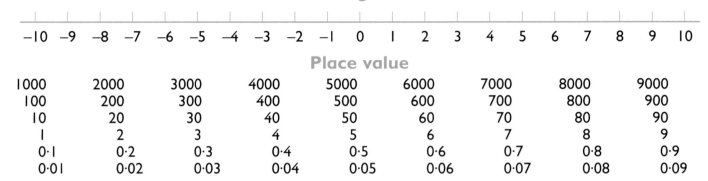

— Multiplication and division facts —

	×1	×2	×3	×4	×5	×6	×7	×8	×9	×10
×1	1	2	3	4	5	6	7	8	9	10
×2	2	4	6	8	10	12	14	16	18	20
×3	3	6	9	12	15	18	21	24	27	30
×4	4	8	12	16	20	24	28	32	36	40
×5	5	10	15	20	25	30	35	40	45	50
×6	6	12	18	24	30	36	42	48	54	60
×7	7	14	21	28	35	42	49	56	63	70
×8	8	16	24	32	40	48	56	64	72	80
×9	9	18	27	36	45	54	63	72	81	90
×10	10	20	30	40	50	60	70	80	90	100

— Fractions and decimals —

$\frac{1}{100} = 0.01$

$\frac{2}{100} = \frac{1}{50} = 0.02$

$\frac{5}{100} = \frac{1}{20} = 0.05$

$\frac{10}{100} = \frac{1}{10} = 0.1$

$\frac{20}{100} = \frac{1}{5} = 0.2$

$\frac{25}{100} = \frac{1}{4} = 0.25$

$\frac{50}{100} = \frac{1}{2} = 0.5$

$\frac{75}{100} = \frac{3}{4} = 0.75$

$\frac{100}{100} = 1$

Calculations

— Addition —

Whole numbers
Example: 845 + 758

```
   845            845
 + 758          + 758
  1500           1603
    90            ¹ ¹
    13
  1603
    ¹
```

Decimals
Example: £26.48 + £53.75

```
  £26.48          £26.48
+ £53.75        + £53.75
   70.00          £80.23
    9.00           ¹ ¹ ¹
    1.10
    0.13
  £80.23
    ¹
```

Calculations

Subtraction

Whole numbers
Example: 845 − 367

```
  845
− 367
   33 → 400
  445 → 845
  478
```

```
700   +30   15
700   +40   −5
 800 + 40 + 5
−300 + 60 + 7
 400 + 70 + 8
```

→

```
     7 13 15
      8 4 5
    − 3 6 7
      4 7 8
```

Decimals (Money)
Example: £39.35 − £14.46

```
  £39.35
− £14.46
  00.54 → 15
  24.35 → 39.35
 £24.89
```

or

```
      8 12 15
  £39.35
− £14.46
  £24.89
```

Multiplication
Example: 82 × 7

Grid method   or   Partitioning

```
×      80      2
7    560    14   = 574
```

```
     82
  ×   7
    560   (80 × 7)
     14   ( 2 × 7)
    574
```

→

```
     82
  ×   7
    560
     14
    574
```

→

```
     82
  ×   7
    574
      1
```

Division
Example: 87 ÷ 5

```
   87
−  50   (10 × 5)
   37
−  35   ( 7 × 5)
    2
Answer   17 R 2
```

or

```
5) 87
 − 50   (10 × 5)
   37
 − 35   ( 7 × 5)
    2
Answer   17 R 2
```

or

```
87 ÷ 5 = (50 + 37) ÷ 5
       = (50 ÷ 5) + (37 ÷ 5)
       = 10 + 7 R 2
       = 17 R 2
```

Shape and space

2–D shapes

    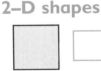

circle | right-angled triangle | equilateral triangle | isosceles triangle | square | rectangle | pentagon | hexagon | heptagon | octagon

3–D shapes

cube | cuboid | cone | cylinder | sphere | triangular prism | triangular-based pyramid (tetrahedron) | square-based pyramid